The Musick
for the
Royal Fireworks

by

George Frederic Handel

Arranged for Piano Solo by
Granville Bantock

Contents

NOVELLO PUBLISHING LIMITED
8/9 Frith Street, London W1V 5TZ

Order No: NOV 915675

1 Overture

Adagio

SEGUE

Paxton

15675

4

Allegro

Paxton

Largo

D. C. al Fine

2 Bourrée

3 Siciliana

La Paix

Paxton

15675

4 Allegro

La Réjouissance

(a) *1st time* with Trumpets; (b) *2nd time* with French Horns; (c) *3rd time* Tutti.

Con spirito

5 Menuet I

6 Menuet II

(a) *1st time* with Trumpets; (b) *2nd time* with French Horns; (c) *3rd time* Tutti.

Published by Novello Publishing Limited
Printed in Great Britain by Halstan & Co. Ltd., Amersham, Bucks.

6/94 (18065)